PLACES, LEGEN
O
THE FYLDE

PLACES, LEGENDS AND TALES
OF
THE FYLDE

OF
LANCASHIRE

by
Graham Evans

TO

WILLIAM AND JOE

O' Windmill Land, dear Windmill Land,
May thy White Towers for ever stand,
Green peace around, blue joy overhead,
and sails like 'angels wings outspread...
Near or far 'Neath sun or star
There is no place like Windmill Land'

(ALLEN CLARKE)

By the same author:

Skippool, Old Port of Poulton-le-Fylde (1989)

First published in Great Britain by
Creek Publishers, 'Tarn Hows', Wyre Road, Thornton 1989

© Graham Evans 1989

ISBN 1 872211 01 1

Printed by Blackpool Printers Ltd, Clare Street, Blackpool.

PREFACE

"I only know two English Neighbourhoods thoroughly, and in each, within a circle of five miles, there is enough of interest and beauty to last any man his life."

('TOM BROWNS SCHOOLDAYS')

This book does not set out to be a comprehensive catalogue of the history or topography of the Fylde. I have simply selected a few places, a few legends and a few tales of the Fylde, and put them together with some pictures for you to look at. Perhaps some of it will bring back happy memories, perhaps your curiosity will take you to some of the places unknown to you.

A lot of the tales and legends are absolute fiction, but not of my own doing! Centuries ago, the Fylde folk, on long dark winter nights by the fireside, would pass on the old stories, add to them, and perhaps make up more!

There are lots of interesting places on the Fylde, and many have one or two stories associated with them.

Visitors, travellers or locals often ask questions such as 'Why was that built?' or 'Who lived here?' I hope that this book can provide some answers.

If the reader derives a tiny fraction of the pleasure from reading this little book as I have had visiting, researching, photographing and writing it, then that is the only reward I ask.

"And all I have writ is writ,
Whether it be blest or curst.
O Remember the little that's good
and forgive and forget the worst"

(AMMON WRIGLEY)

Shipwreck of the Stella Marie *Fleetwood North Wharf, 1941.*

CONTENTS

	Page
INTRODUCTION	11
SHIPWRECK AT THE GYNN INN	13
OLD FORD OF ALDEWATH, SHARD BRIDGE AND THE DOGGY GHOST	17
PILLING, OWD NICKS BRIDGE AND THE PUGILISTIC PARSON	23
FYLDE BOGGARTS	29
'MAD JACK', THE SQUIRE OF LITTLE ECCLESTON	35
OLD CUSTOMS IN THE FYLDE	39
SINGLETON — WITCHES, MILLERS AND BOGGARTS	43
MARTON MERE — MERMAIDS, BOGGARTS AND WATER MILLS	51
THE PILLING PIG	55
MAINS HALL — PRIEST HOLES, ROYAL ROMANCE AND WANDERING SCOTS	57
ROMAN ROAD, KATES PAD AND DANES PAD	61
FLEETWOOD NORTH WHARF, WYRE LIGHT AND WRECK OF THE *STELLA MARIE*	65
PENNYSTONE ROCK AND THE LOST VILLAGE OF SINGLETON THORPE	69
ACKNOWLEDGEMENTS	74
FURTHER READING	75
FINAL WORDS	76

INTRODUCTION

The Fylde of Lancashire (Fylde = 'Field'), is a great green expanse of flatlands, surrounded by the Trough of Bowland Fells, to the East, the River Ribble to the South, and the River Lune, to the North. Well known are its major towns of Lytham, St. Annes, Fleetwood, Kirkham and Blackpool, but lesser known, of course are the smaller villages and places of the inner Fylde countryside.

The country lanes of the Fylde still provide evidence of the remains of the unspoilt old Lancashire. Much of the scenery remains unchanged, the farmers still go about their work as generations have done before them, and the Fylde Dialect is still to be heard in some of the 'Tap Rooms' of the Pubs!

Lancashire has been, by Allen Clarke, divided into two sections. The first section is the industrial area of East Lancashire, called 'steam engine land', and the area of the Fylde, termed 'Windmill Land'. Indeed, the flatness of the land provided an excellent base for windmills in the seventeenth and eighteenth centuries.

If you want to find history in the Fylde, look for it. Make the effort and be rewarded.

History is not 'obvious' in this part of the world. The relentless 'progress' of development of Blackpool has led to the demolition of many old buildings over the years (for example, the old village of Bispham).

However, a search for clues, and an eye for the unusual produces a Fylde of great interest and history.

At the time of writing there is a new enthusiasm for 'Green' conservation, with renovation of old buildings of character for specific use (for example the Marsh Mill at Thornton, being used as a craft centre).

Let us all use the Fylde wisely in the future. Lets look after it, love it and keep it.

1

SHIPWRECK AT THE GYNN INN

The present day Gynn Inn is situated on Blackpools north shore, on a relatively low lying dip of land before the coastline continues upwards onto the Bispham Cliffs. The present Gynn Inn is in fact situated much further inland than the old 'Ginn Inn', being on the inland side of a large modern roundabout.

The Gynn Inn, Blackpool, North Shore. During a violent storm on June 11th, 1833, the landlords daughter held a lighted candle to the window, guiding a stricken schooner to safety.

13

The Gynn Inn (c. 1910). The track in the foreground led to 'Uncle Toms Cabin'. Landlord Billy Snape's ale and food were famous.

The old Ginn or Gynn was a small valley running down to the sea, through which a small streamlet flowed. This stream has now been culverted under the more recent Gynn Gardens and under the roundabout, reaching the sea at a lower level.

The word Ginn or Gynn, is known as a Lancashire dialect origin meaning 'channel' or 'hollow'. A similar word 'Ginnell' describes a narrow passageway.

At the bottom of the Gynn Valley, almost touching the sands, was the old 'Ginn Inn'.

A steep track led up the cliffs in a northerly direction towards the hamlet of Bispham, and the old 'Uncle Toms Cabin'.

The old Uncle Toms Cabin, of course, falling foul of the relentless coastal erosion, being demolished only when in imminent danger of falling into the sea!

The old Gynn Inn was one of the few early Blackpool Hostelries to become Inns for visitors in the 1700s and early 1800s, and was renowned for its good food and ale.

Also travellers between the old villages of Bispham and Marton would call with their horses for refreshment and rest. It was once recorded that seventy-four horses were stabled overnight at one time!

The Ginn Inn was also a favourite place for mariners, especially the inshore fishermen. There would be lobster pots and nets drying over small boats outside. Barrels of salt fish were also a common sight outside the Inn. Exceptionally high tides would bring the waters of the sea up the 'Gynn', and the water would frequently lap at the front steps of the pub.

Billy Snape, the landlord, boasted that "no storm would ever damage his Inn on the cliffs, and that no inundation of the tide would be a threat to the safety of his hostelry".

In spite of his challenge and promise, an exceptionally high tide could and did flood his cellars, the sea water presumably giving a rather salty tang to his beer!

On one exceptional night, on the 11th June 1833, severe storms combined with strong westerly winds led to eleven wrecks from floundering ships along the length of the Fylde coast. In particular, at the height of the storm, at high tide towards midnight, a struggling Scottish schooner from Lerwick was being lashed by the storm towards the Bispham cliffs.

The troubled ship was guided to the safety of the Gynn cove by a candle-light placed in the window of the Gynn Inn.

The waves were thundering upto the front door of the Hostelry and the vessel was guided up the gully to safety, its bow spit almost touching the windows of the inn! Legend has it that it was the Landlord's (Billy Snape) daughter who placed the candle in the window. Thankfully all the crew were saved, given hot food and drink and given a bed for the night.

The Reverend William Thornber was convinced that the crew had been spared from a watery grave by the will of God. In fact the captain of the ship was described as being an extremely strict religious man of tight morals and discipline.

The captain would not allow swearing or blasphemy of any sort on his ship, and frequently in times of danger he would pray out loud for help. He certainly did this on the night he was saved, and was washed overboard twice during the beaching of his ship. He was heard to cry out "Lord save me"!

The next day, at St Johns Parish Church, the Reverend William Thornber preached a sermon to the sailors and his parishioners from Matthew XIV v. 30-31, and presented the ships mate with a bible, in which he had written:

"But when he saw the wind boisterous, he was affraid, and beggining to sink, he cried Lord save me!"

Interestingly, Billy Snapes daughter at the Gynn Inn, who held the candle at the windows, later married the captain of the saved Scottish ship.

2

THE OLD FORD OF ALDEWATH, SHARD BRIDGE, AND THE DOGGY GHOST!

Seven miles upstream from the mouth of the River Wyre at Fleetwood, you will find an old fording point, now a toll bridge called the Shard or Shard Bridge. This bridge is one of three bridges crossing the River Wyre on the Fylde, connecting the area of the Fylde to the 'Over Wyre'

'Dishdolls' Out Rawcliffe. An old toll house on the road to St Michaels on Wyre. An old lady 'Dishy Dolly' would rattle a plate out of the window to collect the toll monies.

district. The other two being the Cartford Bridge at Little Eccleston, and the Roadbridge at St Michaels on Wyre.

In ancient times this position marked the site of an old fording point at low tides, and occasionally a ferryman with small rowing boat. This point was called ALDEWATH, which is of Saxon derivation meaning 'old ford'. It is highly probable that the Romans used this fording point across the River Wyre. The ancient track of Danes Pad led from the Fylde via Skippool to the area of Aldewath, and thence on to Kates Pad, leading to Morecambe Bay and Lancaster across the mosslands and marshes of the ancient Over Wyre lands.

The Aldewath Ford was mentioned in 1330, as there were numerous quarrels going on about the passage of goods via tracks across Sir Adam Banastre's lands at Skippool and Singleton. In Particular, the old 'Mains Lane' which led along the riverbank to Aldewath Ford, and then on to near Mains Hall. This track was obviously the main trade route between the hamlets of Bispham, Marton and Poulton (in those days Blackpool had not been invented!) across the River Wyre, heading for Lancaster. Sir Adam Banastre granted to the Prior of Lancaster *'a road from the vills of Pulton and Thorneton past Skeppol and thence to Singleton Park by a road which led to the Ford of Aldewath in the water of the Wyre'* (Baines History of Lancashire 1825).

In the 1700s, Thomas Tyldesley of Foxhall mentions in his diary, a journey over to the Over Wyre district, where he had occasion to use the Ferry at Aldewath. He writes:

'Saw ye ferry man carry out of his boat a Scot and his pack, a sight I never saw before, being fifty six years of age.' This shows how unusual it must have been for a 'foreigner' to arrive in the relative outback of the Fylde in the 1700s. There was even some speculation that he might even have been a messenger sent from Stuart Conspirators in Scotland!

The present day Shard Bridge was built of cast iron after an Act of Parliament was obtained in 1862 to build a toll bridge.

It was built by investment of private monies, mainly from local farmers and merchants, for a sum of £13,000. The River Wyre is some 325 yards wide at the Shard Bridge.

Interestingly the original Shard Bridge act describes the assortment of vehicles likely to pass over the bridge in the middle 1800s:

> "For every horse or other beast drawing any coach, stagecoach, omnibus, van, caravan, sociable, Berlin, Landau, Chariot, vis a vis, Barouche, Phalton, Chaise Marine, Galash, Curricle, Chair, Gig, Whiskey Hearse, Litter, Chaise or lite carriage THREEPENCE".
>
> (Shard Bridge 1862).

The public house on the Over Wyre side of the bridge, the SHARD INN, was once, in fact a cafe and 'Tea Room', only being converted into a public house in the late 1950s. The original hostelry was on the other side of the road, famous for its association with the 'Shard Horse Races', where the local farmers would bet, get drunk and generally make merry. It is said that on occasions Charabancs full of rather loose ladies from Blackpool would arrive at the Shard for the general entertainment of the Over Wyre young farmers! This hostelry was called the 'THREE BOATS'.

A rather sad story happened at the SHARD INN on 14th August 1908.

A gravestone is still to be seen by the riverbank in the car park of the pub, facing the waters of the River Wyre. The inscription on the gravestone reads:

> "In memory of my dear sons dog, JACK, who died on the 15th January 1915. His master lost his life in saving this dumb faithful friend in the year 1905."

The dog is buried at this grave. The story is that on a day of strong tides, the boy and dog were together in a little rowing boat in the River Wyre under the Shard Bridge. Somehow the dog fell overboard, and started to swim to the shore. The tide was strong, with the waters rushing upstream in a strong gully of current, and the dog was being swept away. The young lad, whose name was Norman Renshaw, leapt overboard to help his little dog to safety. Alas his swimming power, at the age of nine was not strong enough to battle with the Wyre currents and he drowned. The little dog managed to make the shoreline to safety. The little dog JACK was described as a cross between a small sheepdog and a Terrier with a black coat with a large white patch on his back.

This little dog is said to haunt the SHARD INN, and only recently, one of the barmaids described a sighting of him.

Jack the dog's gravestone. Shard Bridge Inn car park. While you read it, enjoy a pint!

She was opening up the bar one early winters evening, and saw a black and white dog scurry across the bar room into an adjoining room. There were no dogs kept at the pub at the time, and there were no customers to be seen! She could not find any trace of the animal in the other room, as he had seemingly disappeared into thin air! A Doggy Ghost?

A drive across the Shard Bridge to the Shard Inn is well worth while, especially for the river views when the tide is in. You may see fish jumping out of the waters below, Herons, or flocks of Oystercatchers. Perhaps if you call for a pint in the pub one winters night, and you feel a little dog at your feet, bearing in mind that the sign on the door says NO DOGS, you will know that his name is JACK!

3

PILLING, 'OWD NICKS' BRIDGE AND THE PUGILISTIC PARSON

There is nothing sinister or macabre about the reference to the lovely Broadfleet Bridge, at Pilling, as the 'Devils Bridge.'

Under this bridge flows the small River Broadfleet, passing the beautiful old windmill, and continuing sedately through leafy tree lined dykes onto the marshlands of the Morecambe Bay.

The reference to the Devil here is entirely of one belonging to lighthearted folklore and fun, commonly described as 'OWD NICK'.

Pilling is a lovely little village, with ancient roots, on the flatlands of the Over Wyre district of the Fylde, adjoining the vast sands (some treacherous quicksands) of Pilling Sands extending into Morecambe Bay and the wild Irish Sea.

The Inland low lying lands surrounding Pilling were and are still known as 'Pilling Moss'. In old times before the construction of sea-dykes, the sea frequently flooded the whole area, causing havoc to the farmlands and tragic loss of life and crops.

Pilling was often used as a convenient stop off point for travellers between the Fylde and Lancaster. In old times, before the building of roads, this journey was not to be taken lightly.

The travellers would first have to wait hours for suitable tides to ford or cross the River Wyre by ferry boat and then have to continue along the marshy lanes across the Over Wyre mosslands (some of which, between Pilling and Cockerham would be under water at high tides!), towards the ancient city of Lancaster.

PLACES, LEGENDS AND TALES OF THE FYLDE

Broadfleet Bridge, Pilling. Where the Rev George Holden (c 1760) is said to have watched the tides coming and going, helping him formulate 'Holdens Tide Tables'.

Shipwreck on Pilling Sands. North westerly gales producing storms in Morecambe Bay often resulted in shipwrecks on Pilling Sands. WARNING—**DO NOT** go more than a couple of hundred yards out on Pilling Sands unless you know where you are going or are with a guide. The tide is **VERY FAST**, and there are quicksands!

The huge area of Pilling Sands, bordering the southern aspect of Morecambe Bay, have over the years witnessed many wild storms, innundations of the tide and shipwrecks.

Broadfleet bridge is the crossing point over the Broadfleet water by the Old Road between Pilling and Cockerham and Lancaster. The Broadfleet is a small river draining the marshlands and mosses of the Over Wyre district. This river was famous for its fine catches of eels, the local villagers using 'Snig' spears and the other odd techniques to make their catch. Once caught the eels would be baked to produce a traditional Lancashire 'SNIG PIE.'

Pilling Windmill, situated on the banks of the Broadfleet near to the Broadfleet Bridge, built in 1808, was six storeys high, and built in a record three weeks by the master builder Ralph Slater. The original buildings have since been converted to a dwellinghouse. Legend tells of a Pilling Farm Labourer, a burly, brave lad, who agreed to be tied to the sails of Pilling Windmill for a bet of a gallon of ale from the old Golden Ball Inn. His mates duly tied him on and the wind blew up lifting him high in the air, whizzing him around in an alarming way. His hollers and screams soon put a stop to his travels, but he was able to sink his beer in victory!

The story of Owd Nick and Broadfleet Bridge, really begins with an encounter of wits between a Cockerham schoolmaster and 'the Devil' in the 1700s. The schoolmaster was evidently far too clever for Owd Nick, and in his flight away from Cockerham, 'the Devil' made three large steps.

The first almighty stride took him from Cockerham Church to the Broadfleet Bridge at Pilling. The second step plunged into the River Wyre channel at Fleetwood, and the third step crunched into the Pennystone at Bispham (splitting it into two pieces!), to end in the cold wild waters of the Irish Sea to be lost for ever. The verse describes the flight of 'the Devil':

> "The Devil was foiled, wrath and gave him a Shaking
> Up he flew to the steeple his frame all a quaking
> With one horrid flight – his mind very unwilling
> He strode to the Brig oe'r the Broadfleet at Pilling."

The crunch of the Devil's hoof onto the Broadfleet Bridge is recorded by Allen Clarke, who describes, after a thorough inspection of the bridge;

'on the top of the right hand wall of the bridge, coming from Pilling, there is in one of the stones, a dent the shape and size of a colts hoof. Tradition says that this is the imprint of the devil's cloven foot.'

I have had a good look for this 'hoof print' and I can't find it! There is a hollow on one of the bridge capping stones which leads to the footpath across the dyke, on the northern side of the bridge, but I don't think Clarke means this mark.

The tale is a nice one, and I don't think it matters a lot if the hoof mark is there or not!

Other interesting tales about Pilling concern the ancient Parish Church, in particular the exceptional character of Parson Potter, The Pugilistic Parson. Legend has it that he loved a good cock fight, and was known to place a 'Half crown on the Red-un!'

The villagers would describe him as 'the best Preacher and Feighter as ever come to Pillin''.

On one famous occasion, during the evening sermon, one wild stormy November night, the reverence and tranquility of the service was interrupted by the announcement of a shipwreck on Pilling Sands.

The assembled congregation, sensing the great urgency of the situation (but in those lean and hungry times probably extremely interested in salvage, after, of course rescuing the crew), started to get up and leave the church.

"STOP!" shouted Parson Potter to the departing congregation, thumping his large fist onto the pulpit "Hold on. Lets all start fair!", and chased after them.

Like the Blackpool Reverend William Thornber, the Parson Potter was renown for his Pugilistic Prowess. It would seem that if the name of God had to be defended, he would have no hesitation in bopping someone on the nose! A case of the parson being policeman, jury, judge and executioner in one long swoop!

Another Pilling vicar, George Holden (1758-1769, vicar of Pilling) originally composed the 'Holden's tide tables.' First calculated in about 1760 with great accuracy, these tables were the first of their kind and became widely used by both Royal Naval and Merchant Shipping. Legend has it that he would frequently visit the Broadfleet Bridge, recording the height and times of the tides.

Ben Alty was a Pilling character who lived in Fiddle Cottage, full of bric-a-brac, violins and pictures of tigers, in the late 1800s. The stories about this rather odd, ecentric, but nevertheless delightful man are numerous.

At this time, the custom on washing day in the Fylde, was to hang out the clothes to dry on the hedges surrounding the house, which, of course, was surrounded by farmlands and meadows. The cool Fylde sea breezes and the hot mid-day sunshine soon dried out, and sometimes whitened, the clothes ready for ironing.

One day, Ben Alty completed the labour of washing and scrubbing his clothes in a tub, and as usual, carefully spread his washing to dry over his hawthorn hedges, adjoining open fields. As usual he went about his days work to return late that afternoon to find that the cows had chewed and eaten his washing!

His comment was 'I wouldn't have minded if they had eaten them before I had washed em!'

In 1660 Pilling witnessed a shipwreck on the sands, during a violent storm. Two exhausted survivors managed to crawl ashore to the safety of a local farm. The sick, cold wet sailors were taken into the farm and given shelter from the storm, being given hot food and small beer.

Tragically, both sailors carried the plague virus and the entire farm household perished to the awful disease.

Until recently a gravestone was visible, near to the Pilling sea shore, recording this tragic story.

Such a place as Pilling, adjacent to marshlands on the coast of a large tidal bay, has always been susceptible to the ravages of the tides and storms. Very often, problems would arise with the high tides of spring and autumn, which usually occur around midnight. Combined with strong westerly winds and heavy rains, Morecambe Bay could produce great danger to local mariners, and other shipping bound for Fleetwood and Barrow.

For example in 1878, a wild January night produced a great storm which caused the breaching of the dykes and flooding of the Pilling marshlands some two miles inland to Winmarleigh.

On this night, the schooner UTILITY was on her way to Belfast with a large cargo of coal from Fleetwood, when hit by the wild high winds and huge waves. The struggling schooner was driven on to Pilling Sands, and shipwrecked. The crew of four somehow managed to cling to the

PLACES, LEGENDS AND TALES OF THE FYLDE

masts, for the sake of their dear lives, and managed to crawl ashore in an exhausted and hypothermic state. One of the crew members, a young lad of nineteen, white and almost dead with cold was taken to the 'Bourne Arms' at Knott End. Hot blankets and drinks failed to revive him and he died in the arms of the Landlord.

Again in March 1696, it was recorded that 'The weight and force of salt water, was so much more than usual, did overthrow and ruinate the Pillin Bridge.'

In March 1907, a gale combined with an exceptionally high tide was described thus:

> "A fresh southerly wind, which had blown for some hours developing towards midnight into a furious gale, and vearing southwest to west. High tide was timed for shortly after one o'clock in the morning, by which time the sea was pouring over the embankment in all directions."

The same has happened, to a lesser extent in recent years during severe gales and high tides, but obviously with the construction of high embankments, the risk is now far less than it was!

If you go to Pilling, go for a walk on Pilling Sands, but don't wander too far out as there are QUICKSANDS! Have a look at the old Church sundial and sit on the bridge in the sunshine looking at the old mill.

By the way, there's a nice pint in the 'Golden Ball' and a chip shop on the way home. Pilling is actually a very nice place indeed.

The Plaque Gravestones.
'C. Dickonson Margaret his wife burid of 1660'.

4

FYLDE "BOGGARTS"

"*BOGGART* (N) Bogy, the Devil, Goblin, bugbear fancied object of fear, false belief used to fear or intimidate 16th Century"

(concise Oxford Dictionary)

The old Fylde was more than liberally supplied with an assortment of horrible Boggarts in all sorts of places!

Very often the home of the Boggart would be a pit, river or bridge across a dyke, conveniently situated to scare off children from the area.

In the pitch blackness of a Fylde night, a villager walking home from the local alehouse, might, in his inebriate state, be convinced of the presence of an evil hairy boggart, hiding in the roadside dyke.

Boggarts were supposed to have existed in Hackensall Hall, Robins Lane Bispham, Marton Moss and Weeton Lane Ends. There is still a pond on Mains Lane, Singleton, called 'Boggart Pit'.

A headless boggart of Whitegate Drive, Blackpool, was described in old times. The story goes that a farmer Greatorex was returning with his horse and cart along the old Whitegate Drive, from Marton to his farm house at Whinney Heys, Blackpool.

He had called at the old Saddle Inn, in Marton and had stayed rather later than he had intended, a combination of factors being responsible, notably too much fine ale, and the meeting up with old friends. He had set out from the Inn, well after midnight on a wild, dark winter night, but did not arrive at his farm, some three miles away.

His headless body was found by a farm labourer the next day, in a copse

Robins Lane, Carleton. An ancient track between Bispham and Poulton le Fylde. Supposedly haunted by 'The Boggart of Robins Lane'.

bottom in Whitegate Lane. He was buried in Marton Churchyard, but for many years afterwards the headless Boggart of Whitegate Drive was said to haunt the area.

At St Michaels, the leafy banks of the River Wyre are said to be haunted by the "GHOSTLY MAJOR".

The Major was an old soldier by the name of Longworth, who used to inhabit the old Hall of St Michaels, on the banks of the River Wyre. The old Hall was demolished over a hundred years ago. The major was a veteran soldier, involved in the Civil Wars of the 1600s.

Legend has it that his ghost now haunts the banks of the River Wyre, on the site of the old Hall. He apparently walks at night, rattling keys and pans, and shaking small pieces of furniture. There is said to be a groove or hollow on one of the stones on St Michaels Bridge, marking the spot where he 'hides' at night. I have had a good look all around the bridge, but can only find evidence of 'grooves' where large articulated lorries have scraped against the bridge! The local priest was once called

Robins Lane, Bispham. A hot July sun bakes the track. In spring it is certainly 'Robins Lane', their song is unmistakeable. The Boggart must have been dozing in the shade on that afternoon.

PLACES, LEGENDS AND TALES OF THE FYLDE

St Michaels on Wyre Bridge. Supposedly haunted by the old major who wanders along the banks at midnight clanking pots and keys.

Sunrise on the River Wyre. 'Boggarts' on its banks were numerous! One was laid to rest in its waters "as long as the water flows down the hills and the ivy remains green".

upon to 'exorcise' the area near to the bridge. A large crowd gathered to witness the cleric ordering the spirit to rest, 'As long as the water flows down the hills and the ivy remains green'.

Upper Rawcliffe Hall (Whitehall). Legend has it that there were PRIEST HOLES hidden away in the cellars of this ancient Hall, and escape tunnels under the River Wyre. An old vault in the garden was supposed to have had its attendant ghost, and a tree still points out its locality. In 1715, during the rebellion, a servant of the Westby's named John Cornall escaped from the soldiers by leaping over the river on a piebald horse, and hiding in a secret stable.

'Where o'er the brook the piebald flew,
Pray, John Cornall what thought you?

5

MAD JACK OF LITTLE ECCLESTON

The old squire of Rawcliffe Hall, Thomas Robert Wilson-Ffrance, died in 1853, the entire estate being passed on to his infant grandson.

This magnificent Hall and surrounding estate dates back to the eleventh century, although the buildings have been replaced.

The infant grandson was ROBERT JOHN BARTLE WILSON-FFRANCE, who became known as "Mad Jack," or the "Rawcliffe Infant," the squire of Little Eccleston. This young Squire was infamous for his liking of parties, outrageous behaviour and the high life.

There are stories of wild, drunken parties at the old Hall. With tales of naked women running around the grounds and servants being thrown into ponds! One occasion brought a party of late night revellers from Blackpool, accompanied by the music of an Italian hurdy-gurdy man and the antics of a young monkey on the barrell organ.

One day, for a wager, the young squire tried to drive a coach and horses across the River Wyre's Shard Bridge, against the odds of high winds and an extremely high tide with strong currents. The wagon careered off the bridge, almost killing Jack and his lady companion. Luckily, he was able to rescue the lady, but the horse perished, drowning in the swirling waters.

The Squire once entertained several of his friends from London at the Black Bull Hotel at Great Eccleston. The Bill for several days of food, drink and partying ran to almost one hundred guineas, and was not paid! The landlady had to take him to court at Garstang for payment, but was unsuccessful as he was classified as a 'minor'. The Squire's estate was still 'in trust', and the newspaper The *Preston Pilot* dubbed him the 'Rawcliffe infant.'

Rawcliffe Hall, Out Rawcliffe. Beautiful stained glass porch.

PLACES, LEGENDS AND TALES OF THE FYLDE

Rawcliffe Hall, home of 'Mad Jack' the 'Rawcliffe Infant'. Family motto being "be wise, be merry. Be merry, be wise".

The Cartford Toll Bridge across the River Wyre at Little Eccleston. 'Mad Jack' the Little Eccleston Squire, trundled across this bridge with a cartload of parrafin to burn down the Old Peg Windmill.

The night of the 7th October 1875 saw the deliberate arson of the old Peg Windmill at Little Eccleston, by the 'Mad Jack'. The miller had pleaded with him for twenty-four hours to spare his mill, but Jack ignored him. Laden with a cart full of parrafin bought from the village stores, he and his cronies trundled across the Cartford Bridge on the moonlit windy night.

Great torches of burning reeds soaked in parrafin were used to set fire to the mill while 'several gay nymphs' from London danced around, shrieking with laughter. The fire burned for three days and nights and was visible for twenty miles in all directions.

The mill, alas, was totally destroyed, and compensation had to be paid in full.

Mad Jack died in 1897, the estate by this time being heavily mortgaged.

His epitaph could reflect the family motto: 'Be wise, be merry; be merry, be wise'.

6

OLD CUSTOMS IN THE FYLDE

The old Fylde was indeed renowned for its ability to celebrate old customs with the greatest zest and enthusiasm.

Perhaps the best loved were the May Day festivals, a survival from Roman times, in honour of Flora, the goddess of Spring.

Poulton-le-Fylde in particular was noted for the grandest of the pageantry in the celebrations of 'Bringing in the May'.

A King and Queen, wearing wreaths and flowers, followed by a procession of the young people of the village, would proudly carry a bough of hawthorn, covered in blossom as a sign of the arrival of spring and the coming of summer.

As the procession passed through the streets, attended by a band of musicians, the lanes were strewn with flowers, and the young men sang and danced. If the bystanders were impressed the housewives would treat them with ale and sweetmeats.

Later on, there would be games, races and bouts of wrestling for the young men (mostly energetic, burly farm boys!) and games for young women. The evening would become the night as dancing carried on around the maypole into the early hours of the next day.

Mayday and the arrival of springtime was obviously a lot more important in years gone by! Long dark winters, with very little travel, food supply, light, and visitors must have seemed like an eternity to those folk. Evenings in the small homes would be lighted by crude candles made of rushes dipped in mutton fat.

The arrival of friends and relatives from surrounding villages to

A 'May' tree (Hawthorn) in full bloom behind Singleton Parish Church. Sprigs of May were traditionally used to celebrate May Day on the Fylde. In Singleton Church there is Miltons Chair, in carved black oak engraved 'John Milton paradise lost and paradise regained A.D. 1671'.

The Devils Bridge at Pilling. Where Owd' Nick is said to have stepped on his flight from Cockerham. His hoof making a dent in the stone.

Sunset across the fields of the Fylde.

Pilling Mill. View from Broadfleet Bridge along the water (famous for 'snigs' (eels)). Tale of a young farmer who was tied to the sails for a bet.

The River Wyre at St. Michaels. A local priest was once called to exorcise an 'evil spirit' from this area, ordering the spirit to rest in the Wyre.
"As long as the water flows down the hills and the ivy remains green . . ."

Mains Hall, Singleton. THM (Thomas and Mary Hesketh) 1686. Another two old stories of twelve monks buried under twelve trees, and an old oak door splattered with the blood of a murdered friar.

'Illawalla' buildings, Thornton (b. 1890s). A Victorian 'folly' originally a private house. Built by Mr C. V. Bradley of Blackpool's Alhambra Theatre, for the music hall star Vesta Tilley.

The Shard Toll Bridge. Looking across to the Shard Bridge Inn. The site of the ancient fording and ferry site of 'Aldewath', leading towards Lancaster.

'Carlin and his Colts'. Often mistaken for the Pennystone. Described in the rhyme.
  "Penny stood, Carlin fled
  Red Bank ran away . . ."

celebrate Mayday, in essence marked the renewal of family and friendship ties which had been lost throughout the winter.

Another famous Fylde custom concerned the 'celebration' of a funeral. I suppose that philosophically, death not only marks the sad ending of a life on this earth, but also celebrates the start of the next life, and all the happiness and tranquillity this brings. The folk of the Fylde arguably, but probably quite rightly concentrated on the latter philosophy, and made the most of the event.

The entire local population, not just the family, were invited to the event, and expected to assist in carrying the coffin to the grave. The people usually assembled a couple of hours before the stated time of the funeral, not to pay respects to the dead but to drink from a barrel of beer supplied by the deceased's family, smoke pipes and talk of their pigs, dairies and crops.

The coffin was then, rather unsteadily carried from the house to the church graveyard by four relatives, acting as coffin bearers, the procession being led by the local vicar.

Sprigs of Rosemary and Box were scattered onto the coffin in the grave and the assembled people each would scatter some dust into the grave.

Then, famous to the Fylde, the 'Dinner of Respect' was held at the local hostelry, frequently turning into a long drawn out wild, drunken party.

Some more well to do families showed a mark of remembrance to the departed by distributing his clothes and effects to the local poor.

In Poulton-le-Fylde, an old custom was for the funeral procession to be received by a line of lighted candles in the windows of the streets.

Other Fylde customs include the lighting of the yuletide log on Christmas Day. The largest log available was set on fire sitting in the fireside hearth. If the log burned for two whole days and nights, then the house was set fair for a coming year of good luck.

The first Monday after the twelfth day of Christmas was traditionally called 'Plough Monday', marking the start of the new farming year, and the onset of ploughing.

On Plough Monday the local farm labourers would drag a decorated plough through the village, calling at house to house begging for coppers to spend on ale. Very often they would be dressed up as women or animals, and would be singing and in high spirits.

On recovery from the inevitable hang over, the likely lads would then report for work with the plough.

PLACES, LEGENDS AND TALES OF THE FYLDE

Singleton Windmill. Certainly existed in 1547 in the Reign of Edward VII. The old miller plagued by the Singleton witch, Meg SHELTON, stealing his corn and flour.

7

SINGLETON — WITCHES, MILLERS AND BOGGARTS

"Some call me witch
And being ignorant of myself they go
about to teach me how to be one; urging
that my bad tongue (By their bad usage made so).
Forspeaks their cattle, doth bewitch their corn.
Themselves their servants and their babes at nurse.
This they enforce upon me, and in part
make me to credit it"

ROWLEY

In the seventeenth and eighteenth centuries the fear of witches and witchcraft was widespread throughout the hamlets, villages and farmlands of the Fylde and Over Wyre. There are several references to ducking stools and other items of torture used to persecute the 'hags'! One of these was situated on the Breck at Poulton-le-Fylde. Very often the 'witches' would be a result of gossip and evil accusation directed at middle aged spinsters or elderly widows living alone. Some of whom perhaps suffered from psychiatric illness of all sorts.

The best known of the Fylde witches being Meg Shelton, the Singleton witch. Legend has it that this woman could transform herself, or animals, into other animals, pieces of furniture or dairy items! Her favourite game was to play tricks, or perplex her victims by changing into things at the drop of a hat.

On one occasion, she played a prank on the old miller of Singleton.

Singleton – Old firestation. The old fire-engine was horse drawn, the horses being 'borrowed' from surrounding farms.

The Old Singleton Windmill was situated a few hundred yards down the road from the 'Millers Arms', on the junction of the Thistleton and Weeton Roads. Singleton Mill was one of the ancient windmills of the Fylde, first mentioned in 1547 in the reign of Edward VIII.

Meg Shelton had been a thorn in the miller's side for many years. He had long suspected that the old witch had been creeping into his mill during the night to steal his corn and flour.

On several occasions he had set traps to catch her, but with a complete lack of success! Every night he would leave 20 sacks of corn in the millhouse, and every morning there were only 19 remaining. One night, he was guarding the corn, and knew that Meg had arrived as she had parked her broomstick in the yard. He counted twenty sacks of corn, but there was no sign of the witch. He realised that she had turned herself into a sack of corn, and he plunged his pitchford into the suspect sack.

An almighty blood curdling shriek, and the cantankerous ugly face of the witch appeared in a flash, but she was away into the moonlit sky before he could finish her off!

The miller watched her sail into the sky under the moonlight riding on her broomstick, howling and screaming, towards Catforth, and safety.

Meg Shelton was supposed to have lived in a cottage at Cuckoo Hall near Wesham, and thrived on a diet of haggis (seasoned boiled groats) and stolen milk. The stolen milk, she would take from the udders of cows in the middle of the night, the remaining milk would then miraculously turn sour!

The old witch was characterised by a limp on one leg, caused by an injury to an ankle. This was apparently caused by an encounter with large dogs after she had turned herself into a hare! Meg had hankered after buying an old cottage at Catforth, but was unable to negotiate a suitable deal for the property with the Landlord. The vendor got tired of her constant pestering, and haggling over the price, so arranged with her a little wager.

The wager was that the landlord would set his dogs after her, and she must escape, arriving at the cottage unharmed by the ferocious canine teeth. If she was successful, she could have the cottage at her price, obviously a substantial loss to the vendor.

They agreed and the race was on. The witch tore off into the distance, across the fields of the Fylde, chased by two very large savage dogs with long legs! The hounds quickly caught up with her, gaining ground on the lands approaching Catforth, and all appeared to be lost.

Fortunately Meg had a trick or two up her sleeve and was able to change herself into a speedy young hare.

She managed to reach the cottage, but as a hare, found great difficulty in opening the front door. The dogs managed to reach her just as she had gained entry and managed to snap at her back leg, causing the injury to her ankle and subsequent limp! However she got the cottage!

Meg Shelton was eventually foiled and certainly met her match with a Singleton farm girl, who managed to catch her.

As Meg was sitting by her fire in her favourite chair, the girl was able to fasten a bodkin,[1] crossed with two weavers Healds[2] across her dress, effectively securing her to the chair. We do not know what happened next, perhaps she was taken, bound, gagged and struggling, to the nearest ducking stool!

Interestingly, it was probable that a character, known as Meg Shelton actually lived in the Singleton/Catforth area in those times. (Just how much trickery or witchcraft she was responsible for will never be known.) There was a Marjery Hilton of Catforth, who was buried in May 1705, under burning torchlight at Woodplumpton. (Note that in those times it was quite acceptable practice to be buried under the illumination of burning torches at night!)

This was obviously not a resting place for this poor soul, as she, according to the legend, scratched her way to the surface with her bare hands on several occasions, and would not settle in her grave.

The local priest was summoned to exorcise the area, she was then exhumed and re-interred at St Annes Parish Church, Woodplumpton, being buried upside-down under a huge boulder of rock.

This boulder is still present in St Annes, Woodplumpton, churchyard. The church itself is a marvelous little atmospheric building set amongst the fields of the Fylde, well worth a visit, especially if supported by a donation of a small amount towards its upkeep! There are also some stocks and mounting stones on the road outside the church.

---

1. Long pin, pointless thick needle.
2. Bobbins.

PLACES, LEGENDS AND TALES OF THE FYLDE

'Meg Sheltons Grave' – Woodplumpton Parish Church. Local legend has it that if you walk around the boulder three times, and make a silent wish, your wish will come true!

Stocks and mounting stone (for getting onto a horse!) at Woodplumpton Church.

The boulder of Meg Shelton's grave, as far as I could see on close inspection, does not carry any inscription, nor indeed do any of the surrounding gravestones refer to Marjery Hilton, or the infamous 'Meg Shelton.'

Did any of this really happen? Was Marjery Hilton the person of Meg Shelton? And is she really buried under that boulder stone? Don't ask me, I'm only writing this book from stories handed down through generations. I don't think that anyone will ever know!

Interestingly in addition to all this, several local pits (ponds) around the Singleton area were said to be haunted by boggarts. An old pit on the Mains Lane, near to Mains Hall was until recently described as 'boggart pit'.

One of the Singleton cottages was reputedly plagued by a boggart from the River Wyre, who guarded the place and gathered eggs. Unfortunately he also 'gobbled up the local children' (I'm sure this must have been near to a deep pond and the story was made up to discourage the local children from playing in that area!) and was to be feared.

Eventually, a priest managed to exorcise the cottage and the 'evil spirit'

Woodplumpton Church Graveyard. Looking out over the beautiful green fields of the Fylde. The boulder which is said to overlie Meg Sheltons grave is seen in the centre of the photograph.

was laid to rest, cast into the River Wyre 'Until the watters of the Wyre cease to flow'.

As I write this, in the summer of 1989, the draught is causing a dramatic change in the river levels. I live near the Wyre, and I am getting a bit windy!

Another story concerning Singleton is found in the marvelous series of books by the late R. G. Shepherd, in particular *In the Country*. He describes the epic journey, on candlemas day 1897 of a farmer called John Richardson. John Richardson was moving from a farm at the head of the Lune valley, to Manor Farm, Singleton, some thirty-six miles away. Manor Farm being the black and white building to the left side of the road, past the Millers Arms.

The story goes that John Richardson's son, Robert, who was only fifteen years old, made the double journey, single handed with horse and cart, no fewer than thirteen times.

He would usually set off from the Lune Valley at two o'clock in the morning to reach Manor Farm at Singleton at about six o'clock the following evening.

On his first return journey, he had found that the signposts had been removed at Lane Heads, Elswick, and he did not know which way to turn to Garstang. Luckily, another horse and cart arrived, in the middle of the night with the driver asleep at the wheel. Robert was able to wake him up, and was given the directions to Garstang and Lancaster.

On another occasion, up towards Galgate, the snow had been falling heavily throughout the journey, and there were drifts of up to four feet on the roads. At two o'clock in the morning he had to pull into a Lancaster hostelry for rest and food for his horses. At this time he was plagued by severe toothache, and managed to find a dentist to treat him, extracting his tooth under gas anaesthesia at three a.m. He was able to continue his journey, through the snow, arriving at the head of the Lune valley later the same day.

The final part of the move to Manor Farm was made by the transport of all the livestock, sheep, cattle etc, by train, from the Lune valley to Singleton Station. (Situated on Lodge Lane – near to where the road goes under the bridge).

The animals were driven up Lodge Lane with the help of the local farmers, to their new home, completing this marathon 'moving story'.

8

MARTON MERE — MERMAIDS, BOGGARTS AND WATER MILLS

Marton Mere is a large freshwater lake found in the low lying lands between the ancient townships of Marton and Staining on the Fylde of Lancashire. Frequently confused with MARTIN MERE, a similar expanse of water, of mainly ornithological interest, near Charnock Richard in South Lancashire, Marton Mere is a smaller, lesser known water, now the site of a caravan park, on its southern borders. Marton Mere was once very much larger than its present day area, being at one time, several centuries ago, some several miles long and about 1½ miles wide, before the land surrounding was drained and dyked, being converted for agricultural use in 1780.

The ancient township of Marton was mentioned in the doomsday book as the township of MERE-TON, literally the 'town of the mere'.

The deep waters of the mere are surrounded by shallows and marshlands covered with rushes and reeds, providing the perfect habitat for wildlife, including herons, ducks, swans and the tiny sedgewarbler (recognised by its characteristic chattering!)

Centuries ago, Marton Mere was literally teeming with fish, and small boats were used, similar to Coracles, by the local people, to haul in the catches. The rushes and reeds surrounding the mere made excellent thatching materials for the old cottages of Marton.

Two waterways were present at opposite ends of the mere, the first being 'Spen Dyke' a channel leading down via the ancient 'Black Poole' to the Irish Sea, the other, was the drainage of the mere at the Staining/

PLACES, LEGENDS AND TALES OF THE FYLDE

Marton Mere. Rushes from Marton Mere were used to thatch the roofs of old Marton cottages, and also dipped in tallow, to make candles.

Marton Mere. Said to be the bottomless home of a mysterious mermaid who rises to the surface in the moonlight.

9

THE PILLING PIG

The Pilling Pig was not a large pink fleshy animal, cured and fried with an egg, but a little black oily mechanical steam railway engine. Such was the nickname applied to the little locomotive with the piercing whistle. The 'FARMERS FRIEND' which ran on the little line between Garstang and Knott End.

The Garstang, Pilling and Knott End railway opened in 1870 at the total cost of £150,000. Funded by a consortium of locals, including farmers John Hayhurst, Matthew Higginson, Edward Hornby, Thomas Salisbury and James Lawenson.

The first engine to run on the line was THE HEBE, acquired on hire purchase, a completely uncovered engine. This being the only engine available, the trains were a mixture of freight and passenger. Between 1872 and 1875 the trains were pulled by horsepower before the purchase of two new engines the UNION and The FARMERS FRIEND, otherwise known as the 'Pilling Pig'. Later in the series of engines purchased were the JUBILEE QUEEN, the NEW CENTURY, the KNOTT END and the BLACKPOOL.

In 1911 the line was extended from Pilling to Knott End, and the formation of the United Alkali Salt Works at Preesall led to an increase in freight traffic and the building of a branch line.

The lines busiest year was in 1920, where 112,000 passengers were carried. Gradual decline in passenger use led to the closure of passenger services on 29th March 1930, although the freight services remained quite busy with loads of potatoes, livestock, grain, vegetables, and of course, salt from the Preesall works.

In 1950 the section of line between Pilling and Knott End closed, but since 1947 only one goods train per day had formed the entire service. This situation continued with weekday trains only until 31st July 1963, under the Beeching axe, when the line between Garstang and Pilling was closed.

The track has long since been taken away, and the old sleepers distributed throughout the Fylde. There are still relics of the railway to be seen, and part of it, near Preesall is now a footpath. The old station buildings are to this day present at Knott End.

> "Way down upon the Knott End Railway
> Not far from here
> There is a little snorting engine,
> That runs at ten miles a year.
> When the engine tries to whistle
> Its all out of tune,
> If you start from Pilling in October
> You might get to Garstang by June"
>
> (ANON)

OUR LOCAL EXPRESS from Garstang to Pilling

10

MAINS HALL — PRIEST HOLES, ROYAL ROMANCE AND WANDERING SCOTS

Mains Hall is one of those places where time seems to stand still. Centuries of history are trapped by the character of the buildings and the charismatic beauty of the surrounding Fylde countryside, between Poulton-le-Fylde and Singleton.

Mains Hall, Singleton. On the banks of the River Wyre.

Octagonal 17th century brick dovecote or Columbarium at Mains Hall. Large enough to roost five hundred pigeons. Killed and salted for winter meat. November in the Fylde was known as Blodmonath, or 'Blood Month' when the birds were slaughtered.

It is situated on the banks of 'Lancashires unknown River', the River Wyre, adjacent to the ancient Aldewath Ford, more recently the Shard Bridge.

Mains Hall was traditionally the ancient seat of the Fyldes HESKETH family, but was marked on old maps as 'Monks Hall'.

Mains Hall was once the temporary home of CARDINAL WILLIAM ALLEN who was born at Rossall Hall in 1532 in the reign of Queen Mary. He entered the Catholic church and eventually became Canon of York, until Elizabeth I entered the throne in 1588.

In this time of great danger, he fled to Belgium for a few years, but bravely returned to Lancashire in 1565, hiding with the Hesketh family at Mains Hall.

This led to the existence of a secret small hiding place and chapel known as a 'Priest Hole'.

In later years his career in the catholic church prospered, and he became cardinal, having been presented with a magnificient abbey and great riches in Naples, by the King of Spain. He lived in Naples until his death in 1594.

Relics of the cardinals stay at the Hall include an engraved window and the cardinals cap.

Two centuries later, during the 1745 rebellion in the reign of George II, the second rising of the Stuarts led to visitors at Mains Hall. Wandering Scots clansmen, from the Pretenders Army, strayed from the main body of men who were travelling down from Garstang to Preston. (Cumberlands Army, of course, were heading north to meet them!) The wandering Scots clansmen, presumably in search of food, drink and shelter, turned up at Mains Hall.

Mr. William Hesketh, having been forewarned of the clansmens approach, beat a hasty retreat to Rossall Warren, where he stayed in hiding until they had gone away. In essence, he was afraid of being labelled a Stuart Supporter, having been indirectly involved in a similar uprising in 1715.

The Scots visitors were indeed given food and shelter, and left shortly afterwards, not before they had 'Robbed a Layton man called John Miller of his clogs!'

Another visitor of interest to Mains Hall was George IV (1762–1830), who was renowned, as the Prince of Wales for his extravagance and joie de vie. He is said to have stayed at Mains Hall for two days, according to Thornber 'In attendance of Mrs. Fitzherbert, who's farmer husband was brother in law to Joseph Hesketh Brockholes esq.'

11

ROMAN ROAD, KATES PAD AND DANES PAD

The modern ordnance survey map of the Fylde is marked with the course of the Roman Road running through the Fylde. This road commenced at Ribchester, and passed through the Roman settlement at Kirkham before continuing its course behind Weeton and Singleton. Remnants of this road terminate at 'Puddle House Farm', south of Poulton-le-Fylde, indeed Roman coin finds have been recorded in this area. The destination of this Roman road remains a mystery, and is still the subject of local historical debate. On Ptolomy's map of the second century, the course of the road is recorded. The destination PORTUS SETANTIORUM, Lancashires Roman Port, may have been in the Wyre Estuary. Certainly Margary in *Roman Roads in Britain* (1957) seems to support the theory that the road continued through Poulton, perhaps heading for the Skippool or Thornton part of the River Wyre, others support the theory that PONTUS SETANTIORUM was situated at Fleetwood, on the banks of the Wyre channel.

There certainly were fording or ferry points across the River Wyre, for example 'Aldewath' (now the Shard Bridge'), where the Romans could cross the river on their way to Lancaster from the Fylde and Kirkham. This track was thought to be along what is known as 'Kates Pad'—a track thought to have been constructed in pre-roman times.

Evidence of the Saxons and the Danes being present in the Fylde (most of which was forest land, mosslands or peat bog susceptible to tidal innundation!), is found in the place names of the area. For example the names KIRKHAM, SINGLETON, HAMBLETON are of Saxon derivation, and places LARBRECK, SKIPPOOL, GRIMSARGH, GOOSNARGH, of Danish origin.

Lych Gate at Singleton Church. The Lych Gate traditionally marked the into sacred ground ('Gods Acre'). The word LYCH derives from the Saxon meaning body or corpse. The old funeral processions would halt with the body at this point.

Tradition tells of the Danes being chased out of the Fylde by the Saxons.

The Saxon women of Poulton are said to have chased the Danes down the Breck (BRECK = 'Hill'), threatening them with screams and waving large pans. The terrified Danes hurriedly boarded their ship moored in the River Wyre at Skippool, sailing away on the next tide, never to be seen again.

On their flight from the Fylde, large numbers of Danes were killed by the Saxons. After a great fight at Weeton, at the 'Lane Ends', the murdered Danes were buried, their bones being dug up many years later. This site is said to be haunted by a 'BOGGART'.

Thornber describes various Danish weapons, tools etc. being dug up on a line between Weeton and Skippool. This would correlate with the course of 'DANES PAD', the ancient track which led to the Skippool area, and the relative safety of their boats!

After the massacre of a large number of Danes in the Fylde, the King of Denmark sent an army to seek revenge with the Saxons. This army

Ancient stone cross base – Singleton Parish Church. Thought to be a boundary cross placed by the monks of Cockersands Abbey.

was said to have marched from Skippool, into the Fylde along the course of the track known as 'Danes Pad'.

This track probably joined the old Roman Road south of Poulton-le-Fylde, although firm archeological evidence for the existence of Danes Pad is extremely scanty.

KATES PAD, on the other hand, has had extensive archeological investigations and excavations over the years. Kates Pad is an ancient track which runs from Hales Hall near Hambleton, to Pilling Hall, across the Over Wyre mosslands, a distance of approximately four miles. This ancient track was constructed of split oak logs, set into the peat, acting almost as a floating road on the boggy marshland.

Kates Pad was probably used by the Romans, on the journey between Kirkham and Lancaster, via the old ford of 'ALDEWATH', it is unsure whether the Romans constructed the track, or whether it existed from pre-historic times.

In September 1950, the Pilling Historical Society excavated the course of Kates Pad over the length of two fields at Moss Cottage Farm. They found the track embedded in the peat, and discovered that it was constructed from oak trees split into three. The wood had axe markings clearly imprinted on the grain, and would indicate that an iron axe of approximately 2½ inches width was used to split the logs.

Kates Pad might have been used in pre-Roman times as a track to the Broadfleet river at Scronkey, near Pilling, perhaps for the use of small boats or canoes. Another theory suggests that there was a settlement on Friars Hill.

While we are in the area of Kates Pad, Pilling and Scronkey it would seem a shame not to mention the tale of BONE HILL a little place near Pilling. Bone Hill is said to have been the place where 'Spinsters with child' from an unwanted pregnancy went, to be rid of the conceptus, the remnants being buried deep in the ground, hence the name.

The tiny nearby hamlet of England Hill has a small church which was built upon an old farmhouse which was demolished. The altar of the church is said to have been situated where the fireplace once stood on the farmhouse hearth.

Interestingly the locals of England Hill still celebrate the COFFEE FEAST, a display of celebration and pageantry by the local children.

12

FLEETWOOD NORTH WHARF, WYRE LIGHT AND THE WRECK OF *STELLA MARIE*

Looking out to sea from Fleetwood, over the stretch of sandbank known as North Wharf, you will see in the distant entry to the Wyre channel, a structure known as Wyre Light.

At low tide, several degrees to the left (west) of the Wyre Light, the keen sighted (or binoculars!) are able to see the remains of the old shipwreck *Stella Marie*.

Navigation into Fleetwood has traditionally followed the course of the Wyre channel via the Wyre Light. The alignment of the lights from the upper and lower lighthouses marking the navigation line of entry into the Wyre water ('Safe and easy as Wyre water' was the old saying).

The great stretch of sands, skeers and mussel beds to the west of the Wyre shipping channel is known as the 'North Wharf'. The channels and gullies of the north wharf bring in the racing waters of the great tide of Morecambe Bay.

The speed of the waters have been likened to a 'galloping horse!' easily trapping and enveloping the unwary adventurer.

The Reverend William Thornber in his *History of Blackpool* (1837) recalls a story of a poor fisherman named Porter *'Who came to so melancholy an end that I must briefly record it. Having gone, in the pursuit of his calling, to the North Wharf, he became bewildered in the dense mist, His cries of distress brought assistance from the shore, but not before the flowing tide had surrounded him. His voice was distinctly heard, directing his friends to the spot where he was, and, at intervals, most piercingly announcing the horrid*

The Wyre Light, North Wharf, a beacon since 1840 marking the entrance of the Wyre Channel.

progress of the water: his feet, his knees, body, breast, were now under the destroying flood.

At this awful moment his ears caught the sound of oars rowing towards him – he testified his gratitude – when, with a bubbling yell of agony, he shrieked out "O God, the water is suffocating me, you are all too late!" then all was still, the tragedy was ended.'

The Wyre Light has been a beacon for Fleetwood shipping since 1840. Recommended by Captain Denham it was 'a structure designed to save many a barque that would otherwise drive unbeaconed onto the sands of Morecambe Bay'.

It was a manned lighthouse until the 16th of May 1948. On this day, the Fleetwood lifeboat *Ann Letitia Nussell*, under the command of coxwain James Leadbetter was returning to port, when flames were seen coming from the housing structure of the Wyre Light. The three lighthouse men, aided by three lifeboat men with axes and fire-extinguishers, failed to control the blaze. The lighthouse was abandoned to the flames and the six men were taken away to safety by the lifeboat. The lighthouse

The shipwreck of the Stella Marie, *North Wharf, Fleetwood.*

was totally destroyed by the fire, and today only the supports remain, colonised by a flock of noisy cormorants.

During the Second World War, on the 5th August 1941, a stormy north westerly gale blew the three hundred ton, three masted schooner The *Stella Marie*, into difficulties on the banks of the North Wharf.

The ship was bound for the port of Fleetwood, full of fish, from a fishing expedition to the Faroes.

Into mountainous seas, coxwain Richard Wright launched the lifeboat *Ann Letitia Nussell* into the teeth of the gale, heading towards the stricken ship. The crew of eight on the *Stella Marie*, were now in great danger, as huge waves enveloped the ship, stuck on the banks of the north wharf.

Coxwain Wright, with extreme difficulty, managed to position his lifeboat next to the *Stella Marie*, close enough for the stricken crew to jump across onto safety. The powerful waves had, several times, driven the lifeboat against the hulk of the wrecked vessel, and the rudder was severely damaged.

With skill and determination the crew of the lifeboat were able to coax the lifeboat back to Fleetwood, the engineer Sidney Hill struggling in waist deep oily seawater to keep the lifeboat on course.

For their skill and courage, coxwain Wright and Engineer Sidney Hill were awarded the RNLI Silver Medal for bravery.

If you want to see the Wyre Light and the wreck of the *Stella Marie* for yourself, please go on the annual 'Fleetwood Wreck Treck' organised by the coastguards and the RNLI, for RNLI charities. Do not venture out onto these sands without an expert guide. You will not be safe if you do not take this advice. You have been warned.

13

PENNYSTONE ROCK AND THE LOST VILLAGE OF SINGLETON THORPE

Approximately one-third of a mile offshore from the Bispham cliffs at Redbank Road stand the Rocks of the Pennystone and the Carlinstone.

Easily visible from the cliffs, as large boulders on the Beach at low tide, these conglomerates of rock have an interesting tale to them. Surprisingly, much of that tale is probably true! The remainder attaching interest to what is an essentially, wild, gale lashed, sea swept section of coastline.

Pennystone Road, Bispham. The Pennystone is almost across the promenade from this Bispham road, about one third of a mile out to sea.

The more inshore of the two rocks, the Carlinstone (Carlin = 'old woman') stands approximately 10 feet high and about 15 feet long, is covered in mussels and is shaped rather like a camel's back. Further out to the sea-line stands the split mass of the Old Pennystone Rock, appearing as two large stones on the sand surface, but thought to be joined at the base several feet under the sand.

The Pennystone Rock is some 200 yards north and west of the more accessible Carlinstone.

The Historian Hutton in 1788 seems to have been the first person to write about the legend attached to the Pennystone Rock and the lost village of Singleton Thorpe.

In 1792 Hutton describes an exceptionally low tide where a number of old oak tree trunks were found, partially submerged in the sand, situated in deep gullies only exceptionally dry during very low tides.

In April 1860 Edward Waugh and the Rev. William Thornber visited the Pennystone Rock at low tide. After a thorough inspection of the stone and its immediate surrounds, and a subsequent excavation, the explorers were not able to find evidence of a 'lost village' or the presence of an Iron ring which was supposedly still attached to the Pennystone. Incidentally the course of this exploration and survey was somewhat interrupted by the consumption of a bottle of finest scotch whisky. As the two rather inebriated researchers sat on the rock, the tide came in forcing them to beat a rather hasty, somewhat wobbly retreat.

In 1893 a Mr. Halstead and a Mr. Bowman found evidence, during an extensive excavation around the area of the Pennystone Rock, of some old oak tree bases and roots. Digging deeper, they described what appeared to be the rafters of a large room of a house, a doorpost, and the crude foundations of a wall. They came to the conclusion that the site was the position of an old habitation.

Hutton had already originally suggested that the legend of Pennystone and Singleton Thorpe had an element of factual base.

The legend itself tells of a huge inundation of the sea in 1588, onto the old village of Singleton Thorpe, which was said to have stood on the site of the Penny and Carlin stones. The Rock of Pennystone was the site of the ancient 'Pennystone Inn', where the famous excellent ale was sold in large pewter tankards for a 'penny a pot'.

The Pennystone itself was situated to the side of the main door of the

PLACES, LEGENDS AND TALES OF THE FYLDE

Pennystone Rock (c. 1880s). The Site of Gingle Hall, the Pennystone Rock marks the position of the lost village of Singleton Thorpe.

The Carlin Stone, Bispham (c. 1880). 'Penny stood, Carlin fled, Redbank Ran away . . .'

hostelry, perhaps acting as a base mounting stone, and was said to have been part of a large Druid circle of large stones. The terrible innundation of the waters in 1588 supposedly dispensed and swept apart the large stones, moving the Carlin stone some 200 yards south and east of the Pennystone. This marks the original of the rhyme:

> "Penny Stood, Carlin fled
> Redbank Ran away . . ."

In 1870 a Mr. James Pearson, from Blackpool, according to Mr. William Ashton's *Land and Sea*, claimed to have found an iron ring attached to the rock, which was described as 'black with mussels', and appeared to have steps cut into the side.

Interestingly, before the construction of elaborate coastal defences along the Fylde shoreline, coastal erosion was a serious problem. The approach of the sea and the crumbling of the sea cliffs leading to the loss of Uncle Toms Cabin, at Bispham, pathways and farmland. It has been calculated that over a period of 20 years, coastal erosion would be approximately 25 yards per 20 years. On these calculations, it would indeed have been feasable that the the village of Singleton Thorpe existed on what is now the site of the Pennystone!

According to William Thornber's 'Pennystone' in 1886

> "The waves shall flow o'er this lilye lee.
> And Pennystone fearful flee
> The Red bank scar scud away dismay'd
> When Englands in jepardie."

Thornber continues to describe the Pennystone inn, being positioned in the centre of a large Druid circle of Rocks. The largest of these stones being positioned against the porch of the Hostelry.

This block of stone had a ring inserted into it by popular 'Thrifty Jack' the landlord, so that his customers might tie up their horses outside. Thrifty Jack was renowned for keeping the finest ale in the Fylde, sold in 'Penny Pots', hence the origin of the name 'Pennystone'.

There is another large rock further out to sea from the Pennystone, called 'Old Mother's Head', presumably a remnant rock according to the tale, of the druids circle. Seen only during exceptionally low tides, I have heard that it sometimes causes problems with inshore fishermen snaring their nets on it!

I have never, even on exceptionally low tides, been able to see 'Old Mother's Head'. There is certainly no evidence now of a 'metal ring' or steps on the Pennystone, I have had a good look around it. Perhaps the hook was placed there by an old wag as a 'wind up'! Certainly it was not present when Allen Clarke visited the spot in the 1920s.

Incidentally, the poor residents of the lost village of Singleton Thorpe, had forewarning of the awful inundation of the sea in 1588, and were able to flee inland to safety. They were said to have formed the present day village of Singleton, (this of course could not be entirely true, as Singleton's history easily preceeds this date), and lived 'happily ever after'. Certainly it was said that some of the old family surnames of Bispham and Singleton had a lot in common.

So, when the tide is well and truly *OUT!* don your wellies and have a walk out to the Carlin and Pennystones climb onto the Carlin Stone (probably the one mistaken for the Pennystone by Thornber and Waugh as they consumed the bottle of whisky), look out to sea, and let your imagination take you to the lost village of Singleton Thorpe. Thirsts now have to be quenched in nearby Bispham hostelries, but be warned a 'Penny Pot' is now a 'Pound Pot!'

ACKNOWLEDGEMENTS

Thank you to the many Fylde folk to whom I have chatted over farmyard gates and in the leafy lanes. To the reference staff of Blackpool, Fleetwood and Poulton libraries, and their permission to copy some of their photographs. Finally to my dear wife Heather who gives me constant support and encouragement, on my wanderings and writing.

FURTHER READING

History of the Fylde Porter 1876

Windmill Land Clarke 1916

More Windmill Land Clarke 1920

Windmill Land Stories Clarke 1924

Story of Blackpool Clarke 1923

History of Pilling Sobee 1954

Shipwrecks in the North West Rothwell 1983

History of Blackpool Thornber 1837

Lancashire's unknown River Mould 1970

Evolution of a Coastline Ashton 1920

Various papers, cuttings, documents and photographs at Blackpool, Fleetwood and Poulton Reference Libraries.

FINAL WORDS

"The earth with its store of wonders untold,
Almighty thy power, has founded of old,
Hath stabilised it fast by a changeless decree,
And round it hath cast like a mantle the sea."
                                    (HYMN)

                              from W. Kethe 1561